A LITTLE ADDITI

inspiratio

- BUDGETS/FINANCIALS
- GROCERY LISTS
- MEAL PLANNING
- FITNESS LOG
- WEEKLY CHORES
- COURSE PLANNING
- SELF CARE
- APPOINTMENTS
- HOLIDAY SHOPPING LIST
- BOOKS TO READ
- IMPORTANT DATES
- BIRTHDAYS
- SLEEP TRACKING
- WATER TRACKING
- DEADLINES
- RECIPES
- ACCOMPLISHMENTS

- DOODLING
- EXAMS
- GOALS & DREAMS
- CALENDAR
- MEDICINE
- HABIT TRACKING
- DAILY TO-DO LISTS
- DIARY WRITING
- MEMORIES
- STORYWRITING
- BOOKS TO READ
- TRAVEL PLANS
- SONG LISTS
- SCRAPBOOKING
- PARTY PLANNING
- BUCKET LIST
- AND MUCH MORE!

CREATE YOUR
Key

...AND GO!

angel
pink

say
cheese

zingy
yellow

mermaid
green

cold ice

purple rain

@muddie
study

@muddie
study

mellow yellow		alpine forest	
caramel coffee		blue lagoon	
baby face		natural eau	
warning		leaf me alone	
lava you		chocolate bar	
sharpay		cocoa powder	
barbie girl		sadness	
hot purple		urghnn	
purple rain			
bad day			
sea side			
hygge			

@ m u d d i e s t u d y

baby gose

caramel coffee

mellow yellow

a	A	ay	q	Q	queue
b	B	bee	r	R	ar
c	C	see	s	S	es
d	D	dee	t	T	tee
e	E	ei	u	U	ew
f	F	ef	v	V	vee
g	G	gee	w	W	double ew
h	H	haych	x	X	ex
i	I	eye	y	Y	why
j	J	jay	z	Z	zed
k	K	kay			
l	L	el			
m	M	em			
n	N	en			
o	O	oh			
p	P	pee			

handwriting

a

b

c

Printed in Great Britain
by Amazon